蕭紅
三幕室內歌劇

HEART OF CORAL

文本 **意珣**
Libretto YAN YU

英文翻譯 **李正欣**
English Translation JOANNA C LEE

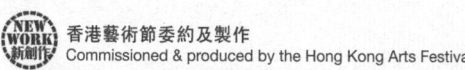

香港藝術節委約及製作
Commissioned & produced by the Hong Kong Arts Festival

前言

舞台可投射自我最優及最劣一面，反映出令人愉悅或沮喪的影像，還提供我們不懂但卻可即時理解的觀點。這是它的魅力所在。

第41屆香港藝術節兩部最新劇作 ——《爆蛹》及《屠龍記》將這份舞台獨有的懾人魅力發揮得淋漓盡致，兩劇包含多角度的對立觀點：內省外窺。作為觀眾的我們，將所有層出不窮的面向串連起來，真相逐步揭盎。

今年推出的第三部新作為室內歌劇《蕭紅》的文本，筆觸溢滿詩意、抒情及細膩情懷，透過蕭紅文學作品所啟迪的靈感，帶出這位出色女作家的生平及作品的全新觀感。

自2009年起，藝術節每年製作、巡演及出版本地全新劇作，直到2012年，共推出144場由香港藝人創作的本地戲劇作品，於本地、中國及亞洲其他地區上演。

特別要感謝多年來與我們並肩努力的藝人，以及於2013年與藝術節合作的藝術夥伴。我亦衷心感謝香港藝術節團隊，讓我以身為其中一份子而感到自豪。還要藉此感謝一直給我源源啟迪的藝術盟友，讓我透過優秀表演節目領略其獨特的奇妙魅力。

何嘉坤
香港藝術節行政總監

Foreword

The stage can show us the best and worst of ourselves, reflect images that delight or dismay, offer views that we may not know but can instantly recognise. That is its power.

Two new plays of the 41st HKAF, *Blast* and *Smear*, exploit this unique capacity, and encompass opposing views in multiple dimensions: looking in, looking out, reflecting reflections to look at how each sees others and are seen by them in turn, while we the audience, complicit in all possible perspectives, watch the action unfold.

A third new work published this year is the libretto for the chamber opera *Heart of Coral*. Poetical, lyrical and richly nuanced, it draws upon the literary source that inspired this new work, and offers new perspectives on the life and works of this remarkable woman and outstanding writer.

144 performances of new works by Hong Kong's creative talent have been presented at home, elsewhere in China and farther afield in the region between 2012 and 2009, when the HKAF first embarked on producing, publishing and touring new local work to premier in each Festival.

I am immensely grateful to the artists who have worked with us through these years, and to the artists who form or renew an association with the HKAF in 2013. I look forward to doing more with them in the years ahead. I am also deeply grateful to the HKAF team, who make me proud to be part of this organisation and who continue to inspire me to reflect upon the wonder and power of great performances.

Tisa Ho
Executive Director, Hong Kong Arts Festival

編劇的話

蕭紅是個特別的人物。

她既是一個對象,也是一個被塑造的角色。

人是複雜的,一個人到底是什麼樣子,其實任君選看,寫一個人的生平,並不能是一個創作。

我希望透過這個作品,看到一種生命的色彩。對蕭紅來說,那是 ─ 故鄉賦予她的性情,她的恐懼和承擔,懵懂和追求。而對其他更多的人,會看到一種更有格局的內在精神。

為什麼一個人臨死前會走進自己的回憶?我們能夠選擇的與己共存的東西,到底是什麼?外在和看似和諧的都是附加,所有情節都成了過客,通向唯一的結局,怎麼樣才能夠衝破內心的一切隱秘,有一幕最自在的反叛?

在寫了很多個日夜之後,「我像火焰一樣衰老」這一句,像一個等了很久的朋友,有一天忽然平靜的出現,幽暗處帶我轉過另一程路途,帶動了生命的基調。

我覺得一個人,最有光芒的地方是在那些成與不成之間所展現出的一種……零散而明滅的東西。

之後的句子陸續湧現,創作一氣呵成。

也許每個人都是在各自的年限裏完成同樣的東西。困惑、對抗、接受、擁有、否定、失去、重新面對生活,這整個起伏,有的人說是掙扎,有的人說叫爭取。

我相信生命是有答案的,找到它,可以串聯愛和靈魂。這就是本作品的意義。

感謝香港藝術節,作曲家陳慶恩和導演黎海寧,能跟你們合作,是我的福氣。

文本 意珩

2009 年畢業於香港演藝學院戲劇學院,獲藝術碩士學位。作品包括:2009 香港東亞運動會《轉體・瞬間》、2010 年一團和戲《夏枯草之味》、2011 年香港藝術節《嬌情》、2011 年香港話劇團《盛勢》、2012 年香港電台廣播劇《我們的十五年》及 2012 年何必館(瘋祭舞台)《大鬧天宮》。憑《盛勢》獲第 21 屆香港舞台劇獎最佳劇本提名,及同年香港小劇場獎最佳劇本提名。

Playwright's Note

Xiao Hong is an exceptional person.

She is not only a character, but also a role waiting to be moulded.

And I loathe to treat her story as a tragedy. That is my position.

Some critics depict her later works as touching upon the deepest secrets of the human psyche. To me, these are not common desires, but notions far larger and broader.

Many of her writings are shrouded by a sense of self-surrender, yet I detect therein a fervent desire for life: she strove to break through in her own maverick and carefree manner. Humans are complex by nature: it all depends on our perspectives and choices.

I'm wary of delineating a straightforward biography, because that does not qualify as artistic creation. And this work is not intended to be an ode to Xiao Hong. I only want to examine her and her alone, to wield words in shaping those brilliant and poignant facets belonging to her.

I hope that through this work, we can appreciate those very colours of life. For Xiao Hong, they comprise the temperaments, fears and responsibilities, as well as stubbornness and aspirations that her hometown and upbringing bequeathed her. Others might detect an inner spirit within this structure. When strung together, an answer to life emerges.

All of us must complete prescribed tasks within respective timespans. Doubt, resistance, acceptance, possession, rejection, and loss, facing life anew, riding the ups and downs that mark existence: some view them as struggles while others revel in grappling with them.

I must extend my heartfelt thanks to the Hong Kong Arts Festival, composer Chan Hing-yan and director Helen Lai. It is my good fortune to have the opportunity to work with you.

Yan Yu, Libretto

A 2009 MFA graduate of the Hong Kong Academy for Performing Arts, Yu's output includes *Passion of Body Art* (2009 East Asian Games), *The Scent of Prunella* for Harmonic Theatre in 2010, *Jiao Qing* (Hong Kong Arts Festival, 2011) and *The Heydays* (Hong Kong Repertory Theatre, 2011). In 2012, she penned the RTHK broadcast drama *Our Fifteen Years* and Ho Bit Goon's *O You Heavenly Creatures* presented at the New Vision Art Festival. Yu's script for *The Heydays* was nominated for Best Play at the 21st Hong Kong Drama Awards and 2011 Hong Kong Theatre Libre.

《蕭紅》首演於第 41 屆香港藝術節，
2013 年 3 月 1 日，香港大會堂劇院
Heart of Coral premiered at the Theatre, Hong Kong City Hall,
1 March, 2013, 41st Hong Kong Arts Festival

作曲 Music
陳慶恩 Chan Hing-yan

文本 Libretto
意珩 Yan Yu

導演 Director
黎海寧 Helen Lai

指揮 Conductor
廖國敏 Lio Kuokman

佈景設計 Set Designer
曾文通 Tsang Man-tung

服裝及化妝設計 Costume and Make-up Designer
鄭文榮 Cheng Man-wing

燈光設計 Lighting Designer
陳焯華 Billy Chan

監製 Producer
香港藝術節 Hong Kong Arts Festival

角色及首演演出
CHARACTERS AND PREMIERE CAST

蕭紅
XIAO HONG

廓勵齡
Louise Kwong

蕭軍
XIAO JUN

譚天樂
Alex Tam

魯迅
LU XUN

黃日珩
Apollo Wong

丁玲
DING LING

連皓忻
Carol Lin

六人合唱隊
A CHORUS OF SIX SINGERS

生命像火焰一樣衰老　呼烈烈　聲聲祈禱

把這一句送給蕭紅與你
堅信它會帶動一切的情

梗概

序幕

南方小島　碧水藍天
記憶走滿荒山　在曠野上呼喊

天亮前，聖士提反學校。此時已改頭換面成為大日本陸軍醫院。蕭紅渡過了她生命裏最艱難的一個夜晚。身體病弱的她被診斷為喉癌做手術切開喉管，卻發現實為誤診。她帶着身體和內心的傷痕，等待黎明到來，生命在催促她終結。

第一幕

不知道路為何而走　留在這裏我也將死去
我看過山坡上飄遠的雲　我摸過天亮時被屠宰的羊

遙遠的中國北方，呼蘭縣。一門喜慶婚事正在籌備，人們帶着期待的眼神等着要看一個女子的人生戲碼。當晚她帶着恐懼和軟弱，從那個小村莊逃跑了。報社編輯蕭軍在這個關口出現，因為一封信，蕭軍愛上了她。

第二幕

眼底流動的火　是熔化的珊瑚
像珊瑚的心　最轟烈只在心中

哈爾濱的中央大街，他們在雪地裏跳舞，歡唱擁有彼此的
生活。蕭紅個性熱烈純真，她與蕭軍一起從哈爾濱，走到
青島、上海……相依而存，認為找到人生所追求的——愛
情。

因為小說《生死場》，蕭紅引起了魯迅的關注。理性而灼
灼閃光的思想給了蕭紅啟迪和勇氣，蕭紅仿佛看到前方閃
爍的燈塔，指引她前行。

情感及人生方向的不同讓蕭軍與她無法繼續相愛。蕭軍離
開，赴延安戰地。

魯迅病重，仿佛預知自己的死亡，寫下名篇《墓誌銘》給
自己。

蕭紅獨自走往日本，在報紙上獲悉魯迅去世的消息。她一
個人在路邊徘徊，第一次，她清醒的感到自己獨立，而孤
獨感亦無孔不入。

第三幕

我像火焰一樣衰老　呼烈烈　聲聲祈禱
一眼一日　一夜一生

蕭紅懷孕了。同為女作家的丁玲不忍心看她一個人陷入窘
境，規勸她同往延安，尋求另一份希望。蕭紅拒絕。她決
定了去香港，無人理解她的思想與渴望。她向着記憶中那
條山路走去，帶着新生憧憬和對自己此生存在的一刻領悟，
她跌倒在地上，站不起來了。

曾經逃離的土地變成她記憶裏唯一的歸處，呼蘭河傳的創
作經此完成。無數幻象，強大的生命力在形成之時也終沿
着江河汨汨流去。

尾聲

窗前一抹白色　月光　像時光　像提醒誰
別歎息　別張望

淺水灣／赤柱海邊，月光安撫着逝去的聲響。海浪和岩石
似乎在對話，回應着彼此的節奏。

序幕

蕭紅：今日香港　海面泛白
　　　人行道上　有人推着帶四輪的板車
　　　馬路吱吱作響
　　　有記者來採訪
　　　問我　為什麼會走到香港
　　　這是我一個希望
　　　懸在空中
　　　斷了
　　　風沿窗　吹進病房

【舞台上一塊牌子，寫着「聖士提反」】
【幾個陌生人，縱橫排列着】

合唱：生命就到終點
　　　活着死去　一線之間
　　　喉嚨切開一道口子
　　　身體斷開一條裂痕
　　　嘶啞着想唱
　　　土地　冰雪
　　　海洋　江河
　　　湧動的　混沌
　　　拋卻的　留戀
　　　像音符休止　一刻一生　顫動的心弦
　　　追什麼？
　　　尋什麼？
　　　守什麼？
　　　愛什麼？

【有人走到台上，將牌子換上另一塊，寫着「大日本陸軍臨時醫院」】

【紅仿佛身處世外，對周圍一切罔聞】

蕭紅：我又想起那些地方跟你一起
　　　每一天　朝露黃昏　眼見耳聞
　　　過去的久遠的
　　　魚在冰下游動　雀躍着　狂舞
　　　江水冰封着　望在眼裏　再近也是隔岸

合唱：窗前一抹白色　像月光　像時光
　　　自言自語　寫字　回想
　　　踩碎了影子　走漫長
　　　從異鄉到異鄉
　　　浪花分不出江還是海洋
　　　擲筆笑　半生冷遇　歡心事未完
　　　記憶走滿荒山　在曠野上呼喊
　　　黑土冰封　被寒天撕扯　裂成一條蜿蜒
　　　記憶沿着那裂痕流淌　源源不斷

蕭紅：（恍惚）
　　　我看見一隻鳥窗前掠過
　　　如果女人也有飛鳥的羽翼

合唱：牛羊下山了　心還守着殘片
　　　月亮下山了　天空撒下一地雪白
　　　問　窗前一抹冷月
　　　答　唱一曲　荒腔走板

【天快亮】
【一聲爆竹，響震天】

第 一 幕

【雪封的麥田】
【一眾農民。這些農民手裏，拿着旱煙袋、板凳、犁刀、樹枝、馬鞭，像一幅凝固的畫】

合唱：正月裏　掛紅燈
　　　漫天大雪爆竹聲
　　　聲聲醉　女兒紅
　　　呼蘭縣城鬧喜慶
　　　張家女兒要嫁人
　　　三尺紅綾揭人生

蕭紅：（漫不經心，不關己事）
　　　唱誰呢？唱我麼？我嫁給誰？

合唱：誰與誰或誰是誰
　　　有何不同
　　　今年正月嫁人婦
　　　明年十五繼香燈

蕭紅：以後呢？

合唱：兩年三載掌心肉
　　　三年五年荒地頭

蕭紅：愛呢？

合唱：漫山遍野　隨風輕拂
　　　愛如春風吹拂柳樹

愛如夏雨跌落河流
愛如秋蟬徹夜嘶吼
愛如冬雪淹沒大地
滿山　遍地

蕭紅：滿山遍地？

合唱：隨手可汲！

【紅一把扯下頭上紅綾】

蕭紅：嚇死我了！

合唱：怎麼？

蕭紅：我不嫁

合唱：呀—？！

蕭紅：人生難道一場戲？人生哪這麼容易？

合唱：人生無非看一場戲
最喜慶莫過　看一朵花凋零

蕭紅：我不能

合唱：你怕！

蕭紅：（四處躲藏）
　　　我……

合唱：（捉她）
　　　怕有何用　　怕往何處

蕭紅：（欲掙脫）
　　　我……我……我不知道……

合唱：人活一場　最重要安心
　　　姑娘，告你一句實情。
　　　人活　不過一場流水往事
　　　鐵打的營房　荒草掠過一生

蕭紅：別告訴　那是我的一生
　　　三尺紅綾　隱約望見
　　　一眼困惑　一眼憧憬
　　　外面世界　還沒開始　如何結束
　　　眼裏一對紅燭　閃爍日升日落
　　　分分秒秒煎熬着　過春夏秋冬
　　　一眼望不見盡頭　一眼已望盡頭
　　　人怎能在絕境裏安生

合唱：人怎能在絕境裏安生？
　　　如何安生？
　　　哪一種才叫絕境？
　　　你憑什麼看絕境？

蕭紅：我……我……我（紅忽然覺得恐懼極了）
　　　千百個聲音在心底　每一句
　　　糾纏着問自己　不敢聽
　　　我看過山坡上飄遠的雲
　　　我摸過天亮時屠宰的羊
　　　我留在這裏我也將死去
　　　我不要……
　　　我不要……

【舞台上也許有一座高台或山坡路，紅沿着山路而上愈走愈高】

合唱：（放手）
　　　生為何生？
　　　求為何求？
　　　路為何而走？

蕭紅：我……我害怕……

【蕭軍上】

蕭軍：一封信
　　　一個陌生女子
　　　她逃婚離家
　　　她孤立無援
　　　她寫信求救
　　　那文字……不不，不是……
【紅在山坡上，險些跌落】

蕭紅：我想要　那樣的生
　　　仿佛觸手可及的光明
　　　不蜷縮　不孤獨
　　　不從窗櫺上隔着冰花等夕陽
　　　那生命　不吹塞北的風　不凍傷臉孔
　　　不冷清　那生命……

蕭軍：（遠遠看着她）
　　　像一個人　奔跑過起伏山巒
　　　她的呼吸在文字裏喘
　　　一句句蔓延
　　　我一看再看
　　　那呼吸仿佛近在耳邊
　　　我穿過馬路　我跑過樹林
　　　在青石路上一遍遍的走
　　　路燈也焦灼
　　　猶豫　好奇　迷亂
　　　不知道愛是什麼
　　　是迷戀她的文字
　　　是佔有她的身體
　　　還是我願意　保護她那顆心
　　　一切早就算好了時間
　　　我的生活在這封信裏　重起波瀾

蕭紅：（看見他）
　　　你是誰？

蕭軍：蕭軍，報社的編輯。

【停頓】

蕭紅：我看見他的眼睛
　　　那眼光　熾熱而明亮　像一道光

蕭軍：我看見她的眼睛
　　　那目光 如驚恐小獸　蠢蠢欲動

【軍靠近紅】
【那一眾農民揮舞着各自器物，如廟會的尾聲，賣力的奏響】

合唱：戲台下敲鑼打鼓　震天響
　　　拉磨的　敲梆子的　整夜通宵
　　　他們拉胡琴　歎五更　並不繁華
　　　吃飽　穿暖　沒啥希望
　　　夜裏梆子愈打愈響　人說那聲音好淒涼
　　　他響着單音　沒有同調和聲的唱
　　　希望總在　最無助時出現
　　　時間一過　什麼事都消亡

【一眾農民隱去，在光影裏幻化成一幅身態各異的風景，如同一組未完待續的鏤空人像】

第 二 幕

【黑暗中，軍摔碎了一隻酒瓶，啪一聲響】
【燈亮】
【軍與紅近在咫尺】
【一陣】

蕭軍：（陰沉）
　　　誰允許你出去？

蕭紅：我走進當舖　賣掉棉被和冬衣
　　　高台上那人　輕蔑臉色的允許
　　　我走進米行　買了鍋碗和米麵
　　　大街上乞丐　可憐討好的允許
　　　我關起房門　我站在窗口望去
　　　等待　焦灼煩悶恐懼
　　　襲擊　收債交租躲避
　　　你問我是什麼在允許
　　　告訴我是什麼在允許

蕭軍：……你是說？是我讓你過上這種生活？

【停頓】

蕭軍：喝醉了　才叫醒了自己

蕭紅：清醒了　才發覺了恐懼

蕭紅：他每朝興奮的走出門口
　　　他每晚頹喪的走回家門
　　　那樣滾燙的靈魂
　　　不知道何去何從
　　　意識在半路恍惚
　　　四周的人們像一道屏障
　　　他奮力向他們揮舞
　　　他的手觸碰到風
　　　沒有回響

蕭軍：人生不只是有愛就天堂
　　　還有街燈搖晃的昏黃
　　　燈影也喝醉了
　　　不知道何去何從
　　　身體在半空浮動
　　　兩邊的樓房像兩扇鐵窗
　　　我奮力向它們推去
　　　我的手觸碰到風
　　　沒有力量

蕭紅：他像一匹飢餓了　受傷的動物
　　　在內心對自己歇斯底里
　　　告訴我　怎麼幫你
　　　求你了　我怎麼幫你

—

蕭軍：世上全是不幸的人
　　　存在着等於不在
　　　應該趁早消滅掉
　　　夜裏徘徊唱難聽的調
　　　告訴我　怎麼繼續
　　　這生活　我怎麼放棄

【燭光或燈光投影在深夜的牆壁上，他們隔着那光】

蕭紅：蠟燭昏黃的影子　和酗酒的人一起搖蕩
　　　一個影子落東牆　一個影子落西牆
【軍突然跳起來，嘶喊着唱一句鄉土的老調。旋律
陡轉】

蕭軍：—灶王爺開着門上西天！—

【軍在那個段旋律中，拉着紅一起踏雪而舞，仿佛
那是寒冬臘月的中央大街，北風徹徹，雪深半尺，
仿佛曾經】

蕭軍：—四十年來家國！—
　　　—三千里地山河！—
　　　—鳳閣龍樓連霄漢！—
　　　—玉樹瓊枝作煙蘿！—
　　　—幾曾識干戈！—

【紅跟着他跳了幾步，軍發洩，甩掉鞋子，脫下襯衫，半身赤裸。紅甩開他，軍突然緊緊抱住她。旋律進入他們的心】

蕭軍：下雪了　凍冰了
　　　門口的雪地　白得像刀刃一樣
　　　我冷極了

【光影在轉換，那一幕跳躍的燭火還原成一抹雪白的牆壁】
【軍與紅像臥在雪地裏】

蕭紅：忽略算什麼？　犧牲算什麼？
　　　我不知道我們是一個人？還是兩個？
　　　空氣隔着空氣
　　　身體碰着身體
　　　他的呼吸　留在我皮膚裏
　　　比我更接近我自己
　　　無論靈魂　還是身體
　　　愛從最遠走到最近
　　　聽不清心跳的頻率

【窗外傳來哼唱，像街邊的流浪，紅附和着窗外的聲響】

蕭紅：（哼唱）……

【遠處，魯迅在另一時空】
【魯迅用兩只手指捏着一隻細小的螞蟻】

魯迅：一隻爬蟲
　　　暮靄中停頓
　　　穿過牆壁的一瞬
　　　我信手捉起
　　　它脆小的軀殼　仿似已枯乾
　　　它突然在兩指間掙扎飛奔
　　　它在不可靠的半空裏瘋狂
　　　要掙脫那未知
　　　千萬次振顫
　　　千萬次吶喊
　　　暮靄的空氣　因此流轉

蕭紅：我在迷霧中前行
　　　看不見未來
　　　斷裂了曾經
　　　不知道什麼在牽引我的一生
　　　千萬個戰兢
　　　千萬種不安
　　　害怕長夜下沉

魯迅：一個女作家，上海現在都知道你的名字。他
　　　們說上海來了兩只鼺鼠。

蕭紅：（轉向看見他）
　　　啊？

魯迅：在地下扒土為生，這個修辭用來形容你
　　　們落魄。

蕭紅：啊。

魯迅：哦。

蕭紅：（看着他）
　　　……

魯迅：給我講講你的故鄉（停頓）

蕭紅：生命像火焰一樣衰老
　　　呼烈烈　聲聲祈禱着　投往死裏去

魯迅：生命像火焰一樣衰老
　　　呼烈烈　聲聲祈禱着　投往死裏去

蕭紅：在故鄉　人和動物一樣　忙着存亡

魯迅：……

蕭紅：他們說，得你稱讚，我就能活。

魯迅：你應該求神，不應該問我。

蕭紅：他們說你是神。

魯迅：他們恨我。
　　　愛一個人用尊敬
　　　恨一個人用遠離
　　　人跟神　一點差距

蕭紅：為什麼恨你？

魯迅：非我族類　其形必異

蕭紅：哦。

魯迅：將來，他們也會恨你。

蕭紅：為什麼？

魯迅：一個北國女子　是異類　也是蠻族

蕭紅：你怎麼做？

魯迅：睚眥必報

蕭紅：小人才睚眥必報

魯迅：傷害了別人，又不讓人報復的才是小人。

蕭紅：普世道理　講純真善良

魯迅： 宣之於口　都是陳情
　　　純真源自　心的渴望

蕭紅： 多憂傷　多絕望

魯迅： 多熱鬧　多荒唐

蕭紅： 我看見你案頭那本《死魂靈》

魯迅： 我翻譯果多理的《死魂靈》

蕭紅： （翻看）
　　　這一夜你會寫到天明
　　　這一頁還沒有校譯

魯迅： 那故事寫他自己

蕭紅： 諾茲廖夫在舞會上見到契契科夫

魯迅： 人世是一腳污泥
　　　市場小丑的搔癢
　　　不知高尚的歡喜
　　　他用檀香的煙雲
　　　蒙蔽眼目　說美麗的人物
　　　人們拍手　追隨蹤跡　送他讚譽
　　　一把雕刀　不刻畫分明
　　　他審判他自己
　　　像無家的遊子　孤零零站在空街

蕭紅： （望着他）
　　　　像無家的遊子　孤零零站在空街
　　　　他審判他自己

合唱： （似遠處回音）
　　　　路為何而走
　　　　路為何而走

魯迅： （看着紅）
　　　　我們向死而生

【停頓。紅看着他】

合唱： （似遠處回音）
　　　　眼底流動的火
　　　　是熔化的珊瑚
　　　　像珊瑚的心
　　　　最轟烈只在心中

蕭紅：點一盞燈　在暗夜長明
　　　　我在曠野奔跑　回頭張望
　　　　當我走進房門那一瞬
　　　　當我看你抬眉那一瞬
　　　　當你背對長夜
　　　　當我惺忪望向黎明

魯迅：人　生而為求奇蹟
　　　有遠方的人　最懦弱最堅強
　　　他日呼蘭　終成絕響

合唱：（似遠處回音）
　　　遇到什麼人　會走什麼路
　　　一盞長燈　指明前途

合唱：（似遠處回音）
　　　春陰的下午
　　　房間裏一抹生氣
　　　投下一列光影　漫無邊際

【停頓。紅有些局促不安，魯迅也顯得無的放矢】

魯迅：你知道易卜生的娜拉？

蕭紅：一個故事的主角？

魯迅：娜拉離家出走以後，只有兩個結果，一是墮落，二是回來。你是哪一種？

蕭紅：……

合唱：（似遠處回音）
　　　河水靜靜流淌　山坡隨季節更換新裝
　　　小城呼蘭　一年一夜　十年一樣

【軍上，拿着一頂軍帽。扔給紅一隻皮箱】

蕭紅：……

蕭軍：我已經整理好行裝
　　　我的行裝只有一套軍裝
　　　這破落的街道
　　　人們在暗夜裏爬行
　　　來回往復　淹沒了一生
　　　我不能像他們那樣

蕭紅：你不能……像他們那樣？

蕭軍：我要去延安。你跟我一起，我們即日起程！

蕭紅：我不想去。

蕭軍：你什麼都不會，沒有我你怎麼生活？你以為
　　　你可以麼？

蕭紅：人多荒唐
　　　在世上尋覓
　　　相隔萬水
　　　找最默契的親密
　　　告訴我，愛是什麼？掙扎、相信、懷疑，
　　　是命令還是鼓勵？

蕭軍：迷亂　佔有　相依
　　　有一天你明白什麼是愛情
　　　愛與恨只一瞬間
　　　漫長的時間裏
　　　我們盡力維持自己（停頓）

蕭紅：（看着他）
　　　我懷孕了

蕭軍：（一陣）
　　　……

蕭軍：那是我的信仰

蕭紅：……

蕭軍：那裏是全新的世界　你可以繼續寫作　我們
　　　的感情也還可以……

蕭紅：（看他）
　　　我是你的妻子。

蕭軍：妻子？

蕭紅：我不是一隻酒杯一件行李。

蕭軍：（哼笑）
　　　……

蕭紅：火車窗望見　冰封的江水
　　　東北　青島　上海　武漢
　　　你帶我逃離了一個冬天
　　　從冰雪走到晨霧　走到雨季

蕭軍：像個孩子

蕭紅：在冰窟裏掙扎
　　　蒙着雙眼追尋

蕭軍：依賴我而經歷

蕭紅：你扶着我的手指
　　　你修改我的軌跡
　　　你給我希望

蕭軍：（嘲笑）
　　　希望總在最無助時出現

蕭紅：這一句似曾聽過

蕭軍：那一句與愛無關
　　　愛太複雜　詞裏唱不完

蕭紅：愛不複雜　複雜的是你我

蕭軍：女人都是深淵（停頓）

蕭紅：……

蕭軍：（看着她）
　　　你不懂待人處世
　　　你不懂炊煙柴米
　　　你在紙上抒寫命途的散聚
　　　你的文字讓我着迷
　　　也讓我看透
　　　那小女子的夢囈
　　　在時代的洪流中
　　　不過是一聲不足道的喘息
　　　你不能經受風雨
　　　你不敢面對恐懼
　　　那一顆敏感的心
　　　在現實裏
　　　有想飛的勇氣
　　　卻又拖帶着怯懦的身體
　　　（笑）女人總是這樣
　　　貪戀庇護
　　　不懂感激
　　　說穿
　　　無非是依賴暖窗前一抹色彩瑰麗

【停頓】

蕭軍：（搶白）
　　　走吧，放心，我仍會照顧你。

合唱： （似遠處回音）
　　　　手風琴在隔道裏唱
　　　　歌聲響徹
　　　　在風雪裏寂寞的街
　　　　一切都成記憶
　　　　三月的風在風裏吹
　　　　春天的調
　　　　快樂的人　不問四季
　　　　悲傷的人　不問四季

【音樂此處轉換成一種遙遠的聲音，像來自異國的音調，此處並不具象】

【魯迅在另一個時空，與紅分處】

魯迅：我做了一個夢

蕭紅： （仿佛又看見魯迅）
　　　　我聽……先生的病快好了。

魯迅：看見一塊墓碑
　　　　碑文上刻着一個人的名字
　　　　名字寫着　我自己
　　　　我一個人在路上走
　　　　我站起身
　　　　我想揮手
　　　　我的手不受控制

蕭紅：説你還穿着漂亮的衣裳，去樓下見客了？

魯迅：我看見我死後
　　　身後一眾卑躬
　　　唱得一曲輓歌
　　　歌名叫做哀傷
　　　淒愴　鏗鏘

蕭紅：1936年10月17號，一夜未眠。

魯迅：聽説歐洲人臨死⋯⋯有一種儀式，寬恕別人，也請別人寬恕自己。

蕭紅：18號，一夜未眠。

魯迅：他們會叫你回憶我，到時候你説什麼？

蕭紅：19號，天將發白，先生像平時一樣，工作完，休息了。

魯迅：於浩歌狂熱之際中寒
　　　於天上看見深淵
　　　於一切眼中看見無所有
　　　於無所希望中得救
　　　待我成塵時　你將見我的微笑

蕭紅：今天看到日本的報紙，聽說你死了。（停頓）我想見見你。

魯迅：我講我的死亡給你聽
　　　是希望給你生的回應
　　　我堅硬如頑石
　　　早不懂柔軟的憧憬
　　　我身邊所處
　　　千萬種荒蕪
　　　飛翔再疾速
　　　也只同黑暗裏踏步
　　　我走　你須遺忘
　　　這一生　誰也不寬恕　誰也不原諒

【魯迅拿出一支煙，慢慢在手心裏捲】
【遠處有哼嚀在異鄉回響，又或是類似木屐走在路上的輕敲，一聲聲，像輕柔的心跳，終於緩慢而沉寂】

【舞台上燈光熄滅，直到黑暗。紅一個人，獨自在沉寂裏】

蕭紅：我在東京　看見街邊　有棵木棉

合唱：白蓮船　紅槳楫
　　　搖到對岸請歇息
　　　長安寺　佛前燈
　　　接引殿裏鐘聲起

第 三 幕

【紅的肚子凸起着，已經看得出懷孕】

【丁玲拿着一杯酒，一邊喝酒，一邊點煙。紅在她附近漫步】

丁玲：一個夏夜在地平線遠去
　　　是不是等來艷陽高照
　　　另一個黎明
　　　一個寒冬在飛雪中淹沒
　　　是不是喚來雪後初晴
　　　另一個暖春
　　　一個秋天在落葉中飄零
　　　會不會走進輕柔撫慰
　　　另一個黃昏
　　　一切經過在四季裏延展
　　　能不能暗示孤獨深處
　　　沉默還想像未知的自由
　　　枝葉掩蓋了往日的迷離
　　　一個段落結束
　　　另一個段落　湧動着人生

蕭紅：什麼是人生？

合唱：經過愛
　　　經過死
　　　經過生
　　　才有感
　　　才有知
　　　才能懂

蕭紅：肚子一天比一天大
　　　一顆豌豆
　　　長成饅頭那麼大
　　　一個饅頭
　　　長成盆那麼大
　　　夜裏睡不着
　　　蚊子蟲子在腿上走
　　　肚裏東西一寸寸爬
　　　我想吐　我在地上走
　　　我想起什麼經過　我哭

丁玲：（走到她身邊）
　　　跟我們一起去延安吧。我們大家都在一起！
　　　我們可以照顧你。

蕭紅：……

丁玲：你在報復自己。

蕭紅：……

丁玲：你懷了蕭軍的孩子，卻和另一個男人一起。
　　　何況你在香港沒有親人，連一個朋友都沒
　　　有，你為什麼要去那裏？

丁玲：在困苦中煎熬　她敏感纖細
　　　為失去而疏離　試圖放逐自己

合唱：在情感裏沉溺　　她依賴溫存
　　　遇到另一個仰慕　　缺少堅強的心

丁玲：她選擇逃避　　又一次逃離

合唱：她沒有勇氣　　再一次畏懼

蕭紅：好像有一種力量
　　　不斷在逼迫你
　　　我向命運索取
　　　即使它不給
　　　我也要繼續
　　　不被理解又怎樣
　　　誤解又怎樣
　　　我一個人走路
　　　我在命運裏喘息
　　　我從命運裏逃離
　　　從過去　　從拋棄　　從記憶
　　　我知道生命孤獨
　　　我向着孤獨裏去
　　　在絕望裏反叛
　　　比在希望裏堅持
　　　哪一種更真實
　　　哪一種更堅強

蕭紅：我想找一個地方。

丁玲：這世界到處是戰爭
　　　這世界就沒有天堂

蕭紅：總有那一個地方
　　　我像童年跳躍着　回望
　　　我和我的孩子
　　　我和我的身體
　　　我和我自己
　　　我像火焰一樣衰老
　　　呼烈烈　聲聲祈禱
　　　一眼一日　一夜一生
　　　我想知道
　　　一刻熾烈是不是純真
　　　一刻熾烈夠不夠永恆
　　　宣之於口　都是陳情
　　　都過去　都古老　都殘舊
　　　都模糊　都虛擬　都表意
　　　都不可及

合唱：江水冰封着　再近也是隔岸
　　　六月的麥芒　在曠野上搖蕩

【紅仿佛又回到那條山坡路上，她一個人沿路而上】
【風吹動荒草，那荒草太高，以至於風聲歷歷，像一種節奏】

蕭紅：我感覺自己即將散去
　　　像隨手　拋入空中　散去
　　　身體髮膚眼耳口鼻
　　　我想看我老去的樣子
　　　不知那一刻怎樣來臨
　　　我眼裏看到那對紅燭
　　　聽到什麼人說了一句
　　　一切都散去
　　　我望向天空
　　　忽然有飛的衝動
　　　那陽光籠罩我
　　　風在風裏流動
　　　雨在雨裏奔走
　　　很多很多聲音
　　　很久都沒聽過

　　　天空是羽毛的歸屬
　　　我心的方向
　　　我看見圖畫
　　　手指勾勒塗抹
　　　一切鮮明殘酷的都遠離
　　　一切沉靜美好的都團聚

【她從陡峭處跌落下來】
【黑夜降臨】
【像手指在天空塗畫，一筆一筆，幻影閃爍】

【呼蘭第一次以場景出現】

【村莊裏的女人們一一顯現，月英、小團員、王婆、平兒。鑼鼓敲響，村莊裏正度過烈焰般熱鬧的夜晚】

合唱：人生無非看場戲　啊喲——
　　　最喜慶莫過　看朵花凋零　啊喲——
　　　看王婆　從紅粉退成黃菊
　　　看月英　呼蘭最美的女人　蓬亂了頭髮裏一層草席
　　　十月的風吹十月的樹　十月的樹木在風裏枯
　　　都麻木　都忙碌　都無助　都起伏　都恍惚

團圓：（白/唱）
　　　小靈花兒　小靈花兒

月英：胡家叫你去出馬

平兒：今年的收成好　多買了一頭牛　牛又生了小牛

月英：小牛呢？後來怎樣？

王婆：一個孩子摔死了　在草堆上
　　　血盡是向那草堆裏流啊
　　　我看着那麥田　一滴眼淚都沒淌　我不是廢物
　　　我把麥子一顆一顆撿起來

團圓：周三奶奶拿着一隻全毛的雞　兩手捧着
　　　要選一個星星滿天的夜　讓我連毛帶皮
　　　的吃下去

王婆：月英像女佛坐在佛龕裏　眼睛變綠

平兒：二嬸用濕布擦她身體

團圓：她的身體變成小蟲的窩

團圓：月英在哭　臉上看不見淚珠

合唱：河水靜靜流淌　山坡隨季節更換新裝
　　　正月十五正月正　四月十八掛紅燈
　　　七月十五盂蘭會　呼蘭河上放河燈
　　　踢踢踏踏向前奔　空中一幕火燒雲

【各種腳步聲匆匆而過，踢踏聲、混雜聲一齊停
頓。寂靜】
【紅一個人躺在曠野上】

蕭紅：天空的雲　從西邊燒到東邊
　　　天着火了　七月的晚霞像火
　　　滿天金黃　滿天絳紫　滿天朱砂色

【一幕變幻的火燒雲】

蕭紅：安靜極了　像霧　像煙　我飛出去

尾聲

【海浪拍打着岸邊岩石，像一種悠遠的呼應，彼此
不熱烈，不慌亂也不急】
【一聲單音，忽然在半空中躍起，仿佛一聲呼喚】

合唱：夜裏梆子愈打愈響　人說那聲音好淒涼
　　　他響着單音　沒有同調和聲的唱

　　　　去年今日此門中
　　　　人面桃花相映紅
　　　　人面不知何處去
　　　　桃花依舊笑春風

Life is like a flame that cannot escape from aging: every moment, it burns in rage and in prayer.

This is dedicated to Xiao Hong, you and me, trusting that it motivates all as they rise and turn and as they join together.

Synopsis

Prologue

Hong Kong, a small island in the south
The sea is clear, the sky blue
Memories run amuck in barren hills
The call of the wild

Before dawn, St. Stephen's College. The building is occupied by the Japanese as a military hospital. Xiao Hong endures the most difficult night of her life. Weak and frail, she had been treated with throat cancer, yet the operation confirmed misdiagnosis. Physically and mentally scarred, she awaits daybreak as her life hurtles toward its end.

Act One

Not knowing what life has in store
If I remain, I know I'll die
I've seen souls floating above hilltops
I've touched lambs to the
slaughter at dawn

Hulan County, far away in northern China. A wedding takes place. A crowd in the village watches the bride, hopeful for a new chapter in a woman's life. That night, she runs away, frightened and weak. Xiao Jun, a newspaper editor, appears. He falls in love with her because of a letter.

Act Two

That fire under the eyes is molten coral
Just like the heart of coral, unbridled
passions burn within

In the centre of Harbin, they dance in the snow, rejoicing in their union. Xiao Hong, fiery and genuine, travels with Xiao Jun from Harbin to Qingdao, then onto Shanghai ... they depend on each other. Hong believes she has attained her goal in life—love.

Because of her novella, *The Field of Life and Death*, Xiao Hong came to the attention of Lu Xun. Lu's brilliance and rationale inspires Xiao Hong and stirs her soul. As if guided by the light of a beacon, Xiao Hong moves forward.

Xiao Jun and Hong fall out of love, no longer in empathy emotionally or in their careers. Xiao Jun leaves for the battlefields in Yan'an.

Lu Xun is fatally ill. Clairvoyant about his own death, he pens the essay *Epitaph*.

Alone, Xiao Hong travels to Japan. She finds out that Lu Xun is dead. Standing alone on the street, she senses for the first time her independence as well as an overwhelming loneliness.

Act Three

I age just like a flame
Amidst fervent calls and devout prayers
With one glance, a day passes
With one night, a life passes

Xiao Hong is pregnant. Fellow writer Ding Ling pleads with her to join her, making their way to Yan'an. Xiao Hong refuses. She decides to go to Hong Kong; no one understands why. Tracing her memory, she walks along a mountainous path harbouring hopes for a new life. She falls, unable to bring herself to stand.

The place from which she escaped has become her only solace. The novel *Hulan River* came into being. Fantasies and the force of life eventually flow away with the river. Everything is inimitably lost.

Epilogue

Is it the moon or time that casts a
blinding light on the window
As if reminding us not to heave a sigh,
not to look around

Repulse Bay, by the shores of Stanley. The moon shines soothingly amidst waning sounds. Waves and rocks seem to be engaged in dialogue, responding to each other's rhythm.

Prologue

XIAO HONG

Breaking waves fill the Hong Kong
  Harbour
Someone pushes his cart
  on the street
Creaking sounds of wheels pervade
A reporter comes to me
He asks me why I came to
  Hong Kong

This is my hope
It hangs in mid-air
Cut short
Gusts of wind blow through my
  hospital room

A sign reads "St. Stephen's" on stage.
A few people stand in line.

CHORUS

Life draws to a close
A thin line separates life and death
Her throat is punctured
A wound cuts through her body
Though her throat is hoarse, she
  wants to sing
In praise of the earth, ice and snow
Ocean and rivers
Undulating, muddled
Cast off, lingering
Like musical rests, heartstrings tug
  at every moment in her life
What to pursue?
What to examine?
What to protect?
What to love?

*Someone approaches the stage, changing the sign to
"Japanese Military Hospital."*
*Hong is unaware of her surroundings; she is
unresponsive to events around her.*

XIAO HONG   I remember those places we've spent
     time together
Every day, from dawn till dusk
From the past, beyond the
     distant past
Fish jump about in a delirious dance
Below the frozen surface is a
     riverbank far in the distance

CHORUS   Is it the moon or time that casts a
     blinding light on the window
Muttering to herself, she writes,
     recollecting
Those lonely shadows trampled
     along the way
From one strange land to another
Not knowing whether the waves
     come from the river or the ocean
She throws down her pen with a smile,
     casting a cool glance, lamenting
     that her wishes are unfulfilled
Memories run amuck in barren hills,
     the call of the wild
The dark soil is ice-bound, torn by the
     cold air into winding crevice
Memories meander along that
     fissure, ceaseless

XIAO HONG *(distracted)*
>I see a bird flying across the window
>If only women have wings ...

CHORUS
>Cattle has descended from the hills,
>but my heart safeguards the
>remains of memories
>The moon has set, the earth is
>covered in snow
>Question: I see a cold moon outside
>my window
>Answer: A desolate melody

Dawn breaks.
A loud boom of firecrackers.

Act One

Wheat fields covered in snow.
Large group of peasants in tableau vivant. Some hold
smoking pipes, others carry wooden benches, sickles,
tree branches, whips.

CHORUS In the first lunar month, red lanterns
        are hung
        Snowflakes abound amidst the sound
        of firecrackers
        Everyone's drunk on yellow wine
        Hulan County brims with festivities
        A daughter of the Zhang family is
        about to wed
        The red silk covering her head heralds
        a new life

XIAO HONG *(absentmindedly, detached)*
        Who are they singing about?
        About me?
        Who will I wed?

CHORUS Who with whom, or who is who?
        What's the difference?
        In the first lunar month, you'll become
        a married woman
        Next year at the Lantern Festival
        you'll give birth to a baby

XIAO HONG Then?

CHORUS You'll be loved and cherished for a
        couple of years
        Three to five years later,
        you will be worthless

XIAO HONG   What about love?

CHORUS   The mountains and valleys drift
        with the wind
Love is the spring wind brushing
        against willow branches
Summer rain falling into the brook
Cicadas singing in an autumn night
Snow obscuring the wintry earth
Filling mountains, covering the earth

XIAO HONG   Filling mountains, covering the earth?

CHORUS   Within the reach of your hand!

Hong pulls off her red head cloth.

XIAO HONG   This is terrifying!

CHORUS   What?

XIAO HONG   I won't wed

CHORUS   Ah—?!

XIAO HONG   Could life be like the theatre? Is living
        really this easy?

CHORUS   Life is nothing but a night
        at the theatre
What's most heartening is seeing a
        flower wither

XIAO HONG   I can't

CHORUS   You're afraid!

XIAO HONG (*hiding everywhere*)
         I …

CHORUS (*chasing her*)
         What's the point of being afraid?
         What are you afraid of?

XIAO HONG (*trying to break free*)
         I … I … I don't know …

CHORUS   What's most important in life is a
         heart that's secure
         Young maiden, let us tell you
         Life is but transient
         An empty barrack made of steel, wild
         grass that is blown about

XIAO HONG   Don't tell me that is my destiny
         The head cloth blurs my view
         With one eye, I see confusion; with
         the other, I see hope
         If my world hasn't even begun, how
         can it end?
         I behold a pair of red candles
         flickering like sunrise and sunset
         Making me weary of the changing
         seasons every single second
         With one eye I cannot see the end,
         with the other I can
         How can one feel secure in such
         dire straits?

CHORUS   How can one feel secure in such
                   dire straits?
                How can it be secure?
                What do you mean by dire straits?
                What makes you think these are
                   dire straits?

XIAO HONG   I … I … I *(Hong is suddenly
                   overcome by fear)*
                A thousand voices speak to me,
                   every one
                Interrogating me, yet I dare not listen
                I've seen souls floating above hilltops
                I've touched lambs to the slaughter
                   at dawn
                If I remain, I know I'll die
                No, I won't …
                No, I won't …

*A raised platform or a sloped path on stage, Hong climbs
higher and higher on stage.*

CHORUS (letting go)
                Why pursue life?
                Why pursue desire?
                Why do we follow our paths?

XIAO HONG   I … I'm afraid …

Xiao Jun appears.

XIAO JUN   A letter
                An unfamiliar woman
                She ran away from her wedded home

She's all alone, helpless
She writes for help
Her words … No, no …

Hong on the elevated stage; she almost falls over.

XIAO HONG   I want that life
That radiance I can touch with my
    own hands
Without recoil, no longer in solitude
A life that does not watch sunsets
    through frosted windows
Not the northern winds, frosted face,
    loneliness or desolation
A life …

XIAO JUN (*looking at her from afar*)
Running along undulating slopes
One gasps for breath amidst her words
Seeping into every line
I read it again and again
She breathes right by my ears
I cross the street, I run in the woods
I walk along the path
Street lamps are alight with desire
Hesitant, curious, confused
Not knowing what love is
Just obsessed with her words
Craving to possess her body
Or that I'm willing to protect her
All is in the timing
My life is here inside this envelope,
    my heart is stirred anew

XIAO HONG *(seeing him)*
           Who are you?

XIAO JUN   Xiao Jun, a newspaper editor

Pause.

XIAO HONG   I see his eyes
           Exuding energy and warmth like a ray
              of light

XIAO JUN   I see her eyes
           With a gaze of a frightened animal,
              restless and alarmed

Jun walks near Hong.
Peasants wield their tools, just like the end of a
carnival, making a huge round of noise.

CHORUS   Sounds of gongs and drums
              resound offstage
           Strings resonate and traditional tunes
             are heard throughout the night
           They play huqins in a simple manner
           They eat, keeping themselves warm,
              having few desires in life
           Tunes grow louder into the night.
              Some say they sound destitute
           A single note is heard, off key
           Hope always appears at times
              of helplessness
           Time passes and everything dissipates

Peasants disappear. On stage, light and shadows cast various contrasting landscapes, looking like an incomplete human figure.

Act Two

In the darkness, Jun breaks a liquor bottle — the crashing
sound of breaking glass.
Lights.
Jun and Hong are close to each other.
Pause.

XIAO JUN *(sombre)* Who gave you permission to go out?

XIAO HONG I went to pawn our blankets and coats
        The man hovered above, he accepted
          them with disdain
        I walked into the rice shop and
          bought food
        Beggars on the street asked for pity
        I closed the door, looking out
          the window
        Waiting, anxious, bothered
          and frightened
        Dodging from the assaults of usurers
          and landlords
        You ask me how I have permission?
        Tell me, what is my permission?

XIAO JUN   … Are you blaming me for what
         you've become?

Pause.

XIAO JUN   When drunk, I'm awake

XIAO HONG When awake, I discover fear

XIAO HONG Every morning, he leaves home filled
         with enthusiasm

Every night, he returns crestfallen
That passionate soul that sears
Doesn't know where to go
Consciousness fades away
Around him, people are but barriers
He gestures to them
Yet his hands touch nothing
There's no response

XIAO JUN   One doesn't need love to be in Heaven
Street lamps cast a misty yellow glow
Even shadows are soused
Not knowing where to go
My body floats in mid-air
Surrounding buildings entrap me
I try to push them away
Yet my hands touch nothing
Powerless

XIAO HONG   He's an injured animal
Deep down, he's plagued with hysteria
Tell me, how can I help you?
I plead with you, how can I help you?

XIAO JUN   We all meet with misfortune on
this earth
Existence equates non-existence
We should vanish before it's too late
What unpleasant music drifts through
the night
Tell me, how can we continue?
How do I rid myself of this life?

Candlelight or lamplight projected onto the wall deep in the night, the two are separated by this light.

XIAO HONG   A dim candlelight dances around
the drunkard
A shadow is cast in the east,
another in the west

Jun suddenly jumps up, singing an old peasant tune at this top of voice. The melody is melismatic.

XIAO JUN   — The Kitchen God ascends
to Heaven—

While singing this phrase, Jun drags Hong to dance in the snow, as if it were a village main street in the midst of winter, amidst northern winds, atop snow that's ankle-deep. Déjà vu.

XIAO JUN   — Four decades of family reign!—
— Mountains and rivers covering
3,000 miles of terrain!—
— Royal pavilions rise to the sky!—
— In the mist are beautiful trees,
branches and vines!—
— How little do I know of battle and
strife!—

Hong dances with him for a few steps. Jun drops off his shoes and takes off his shirt. He is half naked. Hong escapes his grasp, but Jun holds her tightly. This melody strikes at their hearts.

XIAO JUN   Ice has frozen over the snow
                    The snowy doorway is white as a blade
                    I'm freezing

Lights change. Lights cast on the walls change to a blank, white wall.
Jun and Hong lie on the floor, as if it were covered in snow.

XIAO HONG   What is neglect? What is sacrifice?
                    I don't know whether we're one unit
                        or two persons
                    Air separates air
                    Our bodies touch
                    His breath remains in my skin
                    Even closer to me than myself
                    Whether it's the soul or body
                    Love approaches from far to near
                    Yet heartbeats are hard to decipher

Singing is heard from outside the window, from some wanderer on the street. Hong hums along.

XIAO HONG   *(humming)* …

From afar, in a different time and space is Lu Xun.
Lu Xun pinches an ant with two fingers.

LU XUN   An insect
                    Stopping its tracks in the evening mist
                    The moment it crosses the wall
                    I pick it up
                    Its fragile body seems withered

> Suddenly it struggles, hoping to
>   free itself
> It is mad, unable to touch the ground
> Writhing free from uncertainty
> It shudders thousands of times
> It cries out thousands of times
> Thus circulating the misty evening air

XIAO HONG   I walk in the fog
                  I can't see the future
                  I break away from my past
                  Not knowing what leads me along
                  I shudder thousands of times
                  I feel unease thousands of times
                  Afraid that the long night will bring
                      me down

LU XUN   You're a female writer famed in
                  Shanghai. They said two moles
                  have arrived.

XIAO HONG *(turning, she sees him)*
                  Ah?

LU XUN   They dig up dirt from the ground. Just
                  like you, down-and-out.

XIAO HONG   Ah.

LU XUN   Oh.

XIAO HONG *(looking at him)*
          ...

LU XUN	Tell me about your hometown *(pause)*
XIAO HONG	Life, just like a flame, will age and die Amidst fervent calls and devout prayers, it hurtles toward death
LU XUN	Life, just like a flame, will age and die Amidst fervent calls and devout prayers, it hurtles toward death
XIAO HONG	In my hometown, men and beasts struggle just to survive
LU XUN	…
XIAO HONG	People said, with your commendation, I can live.
LU XUN	Pray to the deities, don't ask me.
XIAO HONG	People told me you're god.
LU XUN	They hate me. Love someone with respect Hate someone by keeping distance Only a thin line separates man and god
XIAO HONG	Why do they hate you?
LU XUN	Because I'm different.
XIAO HONG	Oh
LU XUN	They'll hate you too

XIAO HONG   Why?

LU XUN   A woman from the north is alien,
                      a barbarian

XIAO HONG   What to do?

LU XUN   Seek revenge for even an
                      indignant glance

XIAO HONG   Only the petty would do this

LU XUN   A man who hurts others and does not
                      allow for revenge is petty.

XIAO HONG   Our world prizes purity and kindness

LU XUN   What's spoken are but trite tales
                      Purity is but wishful thinking

XIAO HONG   What sadness, what despair

LU XUN   What a bustle, what a farce

XIAO HONG   I see a copy of *Dead Souls*
                      on your desk

LU XUN   I'm translating Gogol's *Dead Souls*

XIAO HONG *(opening the book)*
                      You'll be writing until daybreak
                      This page has yet to be edited

LU XUN   It's an autobiographical tale

XIAO HONG   Nozdryov meets Chichikov at a ball

LU XUN   The world is covered in dirt and mud
                     A clown twitches in the market square
                     Joy that knows no elegance
                     He uses the smoke from sandalwood
                     To blur his vision as he depicts
                         gorgeous creatures
                     People applaud, following him,
                         heaping praise on him
                     A scalpel that cannot sculpt
                     He judges himself
                     Like a vagabond, standing alone on an
                         empty street

XIAO HONG (*looking at him*)
                     Like a vagabond, standing alone on an
                         empty street
                     He judges himself

CHORUS (*like echoes from afar*)
                     Why do we follow our paths?
                     Why do we follow our paths?

LU XUN (*looking at Hong*)
                     We live in face of death

Pause. Hong looks at him.

CHORUS (*like echoes from afar*)
                     That fire under the eyes is molten coral
                     Just like the heart of coral, unbridled
                         passions burn within

XIAO HONG   I light a lamp for the dark night
I run in the wild, casting a
      backward glance
The moment I enter the room
The moment your eyes meet mine
The moment you turn your back
      against the dark night
I face dawn with drowsy eyes

LU XUN   Man lives for miracles
We're weakest but also strongest
      when we look at home from afar
Hulan's name will soon become legend

CHORUS *(like echoes from afar)*
      Who will we meet?
        What path will we follow?
      A lamp casts a light yonder

CHORUS *(like echoes from afar)*
      A spring afternoon
      There's life in the room
      An endless source of light and shadow

Pause. Hong feels unease, so does Lu Xun.

LU XUN   Do you know Ibsen's Nora?

XIAO HONG   The main character in a story?

LU XUN   There are only two possible endings
      after Nora leaves home: her demise
      or her return. What are you?

XIAO HONG …

CHORUS *(like echoes from afar)*
> The brook flows without a sound, the
> hills change according to
> the seasons
> The little town of Hulan remains the
> same after a decade

Jun enters, holding a military cap. He throws a suitcase at Hong.

XIAO HONG …

XIAO JUN   I've packed our belongings
There's only a single uniform in
    my luggage
On this shabby street
People crawl about in the dark
Coming to and fro,
    drowning their lives
I shall not be like them

XIAO HONG   You will not … be like them?

XIAO JUN   I'm going to Yan'an. Come with me,
    we'll leave now!

XIAO HONG   I don't want to go.

XIAO JUN   You think you can live without me?
    You can't do a thing.

XIAO HONG   Man is absurd
Searching all over the world
Across oceans and seas
Looking for intimacy and rapport
Tell me, what is love? Struggle, belief,
        doubt, an edict or encouragement?

XIAO JUN   Confusion, obsession, dependence
One day you'll understand
Only a split-second divides love
        and hate
In the endless stretch of time
We try our best to be ourselves *(pause)*

XIAO HONG *(looking at him)*
I'm pregnant.

XIAO JUN *(beat)*   …

XIAO JUN   That's my religion.

XIAO HONG   …

XIAO JUN   It's a whole new world. You can
continue to write. Our relationship
could also …

XIAO HONG *(looking at him)*
I'm your wife.

XIAO JUN   Wife?

XIAO HONG   I'm not a wine glass,
not a piece of luggage.

XIAO JUN *(in a humph)*

    …

XIAO HONG   I saw frozen rivers from the train
In the northeast, Qingdao, Shanghai,
   Wuhan
You escaped with me from winter
From snow and ice, I emerged into
   morning dew and rainy seasons

XIAO JUN   Just like a child

XIAO HONG   Struggling in an icy crevasse
Searching, blindfolded

XIAO JUN   Relying on my experience

XIAO HONG   You held onto my fingers
You changed my path
You gave me hope

XIAO JUN *(mockingly)*

    Hope always appears at times
    of helplessness

XIAO HONG   I've heard this before

XIAO JUN   It has nothing to do with love
Love's too complicated to be
   expressed in song

XIAO HONG   Love's not complicated,
    we are complicated

XIAO JUN   Women are like an abyss *(pause)*

XIAO HONG   …

XIAO JUN *(looking at her)*
> You don't understand the way of
>   the world
> You don't know how to run a home
> You describe people's meeting
>   and parting
> Your words so beguiled me
> They also let me see through
> A woman's mad ravings
> Against the tide of time
> Are but an insignificant gasp
> You cannot withstand wind and rain
> You're afraid of fear itself
> Your sensitive heart
> In reality
> Yearns to soar
> Yet it's dragged down by a
>   cowardly body
> *(laughs)*
> Women: they crave protection yet
>   they're ungrateful. They only
>   cherish the abundance of
>   colours and warmth in front of
>   their windows

Pause.

XIAO JUN *(speaking)*
> Go, don't worry. I'll still take care
>   of you.

CHORUS *(like echoes from afar)*

> On a neighboring street,
> an accordion plays
> Over a loud singing voice
> In that windy, snowy, lonely street
> Everything has become a memory
> In the third month, the wind contains
> Melodies of spring
> People who are happy care not about
> the season
> People who are sad care not about
> the season

Music becomes faint and distant, as if from an unspecified, foreign land.
Lu Xun in a different time and space from Hong.

LU XUN I had a dream

XIAO HONG *(as if she sees Lu Xun)*

> I hear … you'll soon recover.

LU XUN
> I see a tombstone
> With an engraved name
> The name is my own
> I walk along on a path
> I rise
> I want to wave my hands
> But I cannot control them

XIAO HONG They said you were wearing very nice
clothes, about to greet guests below

LU XUN	After my death, I see Crowds gathering with their heads 　　bowed low to pay respect They sing an elegy Entitled Sorrow Desolate, resounding
HON	October 17th 1936, a sleepless night.
LU XUN	I hear Europeans, at their deathbed … 　　go through a ritual of forgiveness: 　　forgiving others and asking for 　　forgiveness
XIAO HONG	18th, a sleepless night.
LU XUN	They'll ask you for your recollections. 　　What will you say?
XIAO HONG	19th, dawn. As usual, you finished 　　your work and took a rest.
LU XUN	Feeling the chills amidst 　　passionate music Seeing the abyss in the sky Everything I see becomes nought Finding salvation out of having 　　nothing to hope for When I return to dust, you'll see 　　me smiling
XIAO HONG	Papers in Japan reported that you're 　　dead. *(Pause)* I want to see you.

LU XUN   Let me tell you about my death
It is hope that in return gives you life
I'm sturdy like a stone
I have no dreams about fanciful desires
Where I am
Desolation rules
No matter how rapidly one soars
It's like walking in the dark
I must take leave, you must forget me
In this life, no one pardons and
   no one forgives

Lu Xun brings out a cigarette, he rolls it in his hand.
From afar there's sound of a foreign land, or perhaps
the sound of wooden clogs. These sounds are like faint
heartbeats as they slow down and disappear.
Lights out on stage until total darkness. Hong is alone,
silent.

XIAO HONG   There's a kapok tree on the street
in Tokyo

CHORUS   A boat with a white sail and red oars
When you reach the other side of the
   bank, take a rest
Chang'an Temple, a lamp in front of
   Buddha's statue
Bells toll before the altar

Act Three

Hong's pregnant, her belly bulging.
Ding Ling is sipping wine, with a glass in hand. She's
also smoking. Hong walks beside her.

DING LING　　A summer night disappears from
　　　　　　　　　the horizon
　　　　　　　Will the sun shine high?
　　　　　　　Another dawn
　　　　　　　A cold winter is submerged by
　　　　　　　　　snow drifts
　　　　　　　Will the sun emerge after the snow?
　　　　　　　Another warm spring
　　　　　　　Autumn drifts about with
　　　　　　　　　falling leaves
　　　　　　　Will there be gentle comfort?
　　　　　　　Another dusk
　　　　　　　Everything is extended by the
　　　　　　　　　changing seasons
　　　　　　　Does it hint at that depth of loneliness
　　　　　　　A silence that imagines as-yet-
　　　　　　　　　unknown freedom?
　　　　　　　Branches and leaves cover up
　　　　　　　　　confusions of the past
　　　　　　　An episode draws to a close
　　　　　　　Another episode is about to
　　　　　　　　　invigorate life

XIAO HONG　　What is life?

CHORUS　　　Through love
　　　　　　　Through death
　　　　　　　Through birth
　　　　　　　There's feeling
　　　　　　　There's knowing
　　　　　　　There's understanding

XIAO HONG   A belly that grows day by day
A pea
Grows as large as a steamed bun
A steamed bun
Grows as large as a basin
I can't sleep at night
Mosquitoes and insects crawl on
my legs
What's inside my belly inches along
I want to vomit, I walk on the ground
I think about my experiences, I cry

DING LING (*approaching her side*)
Come with us to Yan'an.
We can all gather there.
We can take care of you.

XIAO HONG   …

DING LING   You're taking revenge on yourself.

XIAO HONG   …

DING LING   You're bearing Xiao Jun's baby,
yet you're with another man.
You have no relatives in Hong Kong,
not even a friend. Why do you
want to go there?

DING LING   Suffering bitter hardships, she's
sensitive and frail
She distances herself because of her
loss, banishing herself

CHORUS Drowned in emotions, she relies
        on comfort
She met another who admires her,
        yet she lacks steadfastness

DING LING She has chosen avoidance and escape

CHORUS She isn't brave, she's fearful again

XIAO HONG As if there's a power
That incessantly exerts pressure
        on you
I take from fate
Even if it doesn't render
I must continue
So what if no one understands me?
So what if I'm misunderstood?
I walk alone
Gasping for breath in my fate
I escape from it
From the past, from desertion,
        from memory
I understand life is lonely
I plunge into loneliness
I revolt from despair
Compared with perseverance in hope
Which is more real?
Which is more steadfast?

XIAO HONG I want to find a place

DING LING War is everywhere
There's no Heaven on this earth

XIAO HONG There has to be a place
      Where I can look back, spirited as
       in my youth
      Where my child and I
      My body and I
      Myself and I
      I age just like a flame
      Amidst fervent calls and
       devout prayers
      With one glance, a day passes
      With one night, a life passes
      I want to know this:
      Can a moment of passion be pure?
      Can a moment of passion
       be everlasting?
      What's spoken are but trite tales
      Past, old, broken
      Blurred, abstract, superficial
      Far from our reach

CHORUS / LU XUN (*like echoes from afar*)
      We're weakest but also strongest
       when we look at home from afar

CHORUS Below the frozen surface is a
       riverbank far in the distance
      Wheat stalks wave in the fields in June

As if Hong is on the mountain slope, climbing up on her own.
Winds beat against wild grass, creating a steady rhythm.

XIAO HONG   I feel I'm about to dissipate
Just by the sleight of a hand,
   thrown in the air, scattered
My body, skin, my sensory organs
I want to see my face as I grow old
I don't know how that moment
   will arrive
I still see that pair of red candles
I still hear those people speaking
Everything vanishes
I look up to the sky
Suddenly overcome by an urge to fly
The sun encircles me
Winds flow within winds
Rain rushes by in the rain
A multitude of sounds
That I haven't heard for a long time

The sky is where feathers
   found solace
The direction of my heart
I see drawings
How the finger moves with strokes
   and paints
All that is fresh and cruel
   become distant
All that is calm and beautiful gather

She falls from the cliff.
The dark night descends.
Just like a finger drawing in the air, stroke by stroke, a
mirage glistens.
For the time, Hulan appears on the stage.
Women in the village appear, one by one: Yueying, Xiao

Tuanyuan, Granny Wang, Ping'er. There are sounds of gongs and cymbals; it is a festive night in the village.

CHORUS
Life is but a night at the theatre,
    heiyo —
It's heartening to see a flower wither,
    heiyo —
Look at Granny Wang; she's aged
    from a blooming rose to yellow
    chrysanthemum
Look at Yueying, the prettiest woman
    in Hulan, with her messy hair
As the autumn winds blow,
    autumn trees wither
Numb, busy, helpless, undulating,
    absent-minded

TUANYUAN *(dialogue/singing)*
Little Blossom, Little Blossom

YUEYING
The Hu Family asks for your help

PING'ER
We had a good harvest this year.
    We bought an extra cow that has
    begotten a calf

YUEYING
What happened to the calf?

GRANNY WANG
A child fell to his death,
    amongst the hay.
His blood flowed into the haystack
I look at the fields without shedding
    a single tear. I'm not useless.
    I picked up every grain,
    grain by grain

TUANYUAN   Granny Zhou holds onto a feathered
                        chicken with her two hands
                She wants to pick a starry night to
                        feed me this fowl

GRANNY WANG   Yueying is like the Buddha sitting
                        at the altar, her eyes turning green

PING'ER   Second Aunt used a wet cloth to wipe
                        her body

TUANYUAN   Her body became a haven for
                        small insects

TUANYUAN   Yueying cries, but there's no tear on
                        her face

CHORUS   The brook flows without a sound,
                        the hills change according to
                        the seasons
                On the 15th day of the first lunar
                        month, 18th day of the fourth
                        month, lanterns are hung
                During the Ghost Festival,
                        lanterns float along Hulan River
                They rush forward with much aplomb.
                        Clouds appear as if caught on fire

The sound of footsteps and other noise. They all stop.
Silence.
Hong lies in an open field, alone.

XIAO HONG   From the west,
        clouds catch fire eastward
    At dusk in the seventh month,
        the sky is aflame
    Filled with golden yellow and reddish
        purple, the sky is covered
        in cinnabar

Clouds appear as if they are on fire.

XIAO HONG   Tranquil like the mist and smoke.
        Let me fly

Epilogue

Waves beat against rocks, just like calls and responses
from afar. They are peaceful, orderly and unhurried.
A single sound bursts forth, as if jumping in mid air,
like a call.

CHORUS   Tunes grow louder into the night.
                      Some say they sound destitute
                  A single note is heard, off key

                  On this day last year in this home
                  Red plum blossoms matched people's
                      joy therein
                  Who knew where these people
                      have gone?
                  But red plum blossoms still smile,
                      greeting the spring breeze

香港藝術節簡介

香港藝術節成立於1972年，為國際藝壇重要的表演藝術節之一。每年均帶來約170場由本地、亞洲和世界頂尖藝人及團隊精心製作的表演。藝術節的節目色色俱備，既顧及古典傳統口味，亦具備新穎創意和香港難得一見的表演形式，每屆入場觀眾人次超越150,000，其中藝術節青少年之友會員佔19,000人次。近年，藝術節與亞洲區內其他藝術節積極合作，孕育新作，與享譽國際的藝術機構聯合委約全新作品，並支持不同領域的藝術家進行跨區跨媒體的合作。經過40年的發展，今天的藝術節不論在表演藝人數目、演出水平、節目種類各方面，均為本地藝壇之最。

The Hong Kong Arts Festival

The Hong Kong Arts Festival, first established in 1972, presents some 170 performances and events by top international, regional, national and local talent during February and March every year. The eclectic mix of classical and contemporary works cater to an audience of over 150,000 including 19,000 participants of the Festival's Young Friends Scheme. The Festival also commissions, produces and publishes new works independently or in collaboration with international partners. Festival information is available at www.hk.artsfestval.org.

出版 Published by：香港藝術節協會有限公司 Hong Kong Arts Festival Society Limited
本刊內容，未經許可，不得轉載。 Reproduction in whole or in part without written permission is strictly prohibited.

督印人 Publisher	何嘉坤 Tisa Ho
主編 Editor	蘇國雲 So Kwok-wan
執行編輯 Executive Editor	鄺潔冰 Cabbie Kwong
助理編輯 Assistant Editor	李宛虹 Lei Yuen-hung
平面設計 排版 Designer	梁佩琼 Polly Leung
出版 Published by	香港藝術節協會有限公司 Hong Kong Arts Festival Society Limited
印刷 Printer	稜創意有限公司 Prism Creation Ltd.
版次 Edition	2013 年 3 月初版 1st edition in March 2013
書號 / ISBN	978-988-16056-2-7
定價 / Price	港幣 HK$100
版權垂詢 Copyright Enquiry	香港藝術節協會有限公司 Hong Kong Arts Festival Society Limited

香港灣仔港灣道二號 12 字樓
12/F, 2 Harbour Road, Wan Chai, Hong Kong
電話 Tel：2824 3555
傳真 Fax：2824 3798, 2824 3722
網頁 Website：www.hk.artsfestival.org
電郵 Email：afgen@hkaf.org